MW00964780

Vintage 93

League of Canadian Poets

National Poetry Contest

Over 15,000 poems have been entered in the League of Canadian Poets' National Poetry Contest since it began in 1987. These poems have shown the diverse range of poetic styles as well as how active the poetry community is in this country. Who says poetry is a dying art?

As the largest competition in the country, the top 50 poems are gathered into an anthology each year. From these poems, the top three are chosen and cash prizes of $1,000, $750 and $500 are awarded.

Poems entered in the contest are unpublished and no longer than 75 lines. All entries must be typed, single-sided on plain 8 1/2" x 11" paper. As the contest is judged blind by a jury of poets, the author's name must not appear on the poem, but be submitted on separate sheet, along with an address and phone number and the titles of all poems entered. Copyright remains with the poet, but winners are asked to allow for the first rights to print their work.

There is an entry fee for each poem and payment, either by cheque or money order in Canadian funds, should be included with the submissions. Deadline for the entries is January 31st of each year. Winners are announced at the LCP's Annual General Meeting.

Since the competition's inception, the winners have been:

1988 1st poem: Michael Redhill
2nd poem: Sharon Thesen
3rd poem: Cornelia Hoogland

1989 1st poem: Elisabeth Harvor
tied: Elyse Yates St. George
tied: Patricia Young

1990 1st poem: Diana Brebner
2nd poem: Blaine Marchand
3rd poem: D.J. Eastwood

1991 1st poem: Elisabeth Harvor
2nd poem: David Margoshes
3rd poem: Debbie Fersht

1992 1st poem: Nadine McInnis
2nd poem: Stan Rogal
3rd poem: Louise B. Halfe

1993 1st poem: Joy Kirstin
2nd poem: Patricia Young
3rd poem: Gabriele Guenther

For more information, please contact the League of Canadian Poets,
54 Wolseley Street, 3rd floor, Toronto, Ontario, M5T 1A5, tel.: (416) 504-1657.

League of Canadian Poets

National Poetry Contest

Quarry Press

In honour of the poetry of
Roy Kiyooka and Tom Marshall.

Canadian Cataloguing in Publication Data

Vintage 93, League of Canadian Poets

ISBN 1-55082-122-9

1. Canadian poetry (English) — 20th century.
I. Marchand, Blaine, 1949-

PS8279.V553 1994 C811'.5408 C94-900457-X PR9195.25.V46 1994

Cover art entitled "Form Complex #1" by Roy Kiyooka,
reproduced by permission from the Collection of the Canada Council Art Bank.
Design Consultant: Keith Abraham.
Printed and bound in Canada by Webcom Limited, Toronto, Ontario.

Published by **Quarry Press Inc.,**
P.O. Box 1061, Kingston, Ontario K7L 4Y5.

Sixth National Poetry Contest
Prize Winners

First Prize
Joy Kirstin
"7:16"

Second Prize
Patricia Young
"The Origins of the Kiss"

Third Prize
Gabriele Guenther
"Oil of Fear"

Contents

Preface

It is a pleasure to introduce you to *Vintage 93* containing the top-ranked fifty poems, selected from the submissions, by League members and other poets, to the League of Canadian Poets 1993 National Poetry Contest.

For too many years I have, as a member of the League's executive, watched poets as though I were sitting at the foot of a tree, looking up: I saw branches and twigs and leaves, curves and twists and silver undersides. I kept track of poets' ever-changing addresses, the titles of their books, their performances in schools and coffee houses, their prizes and problems, and, of course, their dues. There hardly was time to keep track of their poems, or anyone else's for that matter. At first I intended to read at least one book by every member of the League, yet that goal proved unrealistic — I felt virtuous if I found time to read the books of my closest associates! But reading the anthologies that have come out of the League's annual National Poetry Contests has not only been possible, it has been rewarding, and a great pleasure. What livelier way than this, to make new friends, and get re-acquainted with the old?

In the present anthology, first-prize winner Joy Kirstin's "7:16" speaks of a woman's sudden intimation of her lover's death on the other side of the world, while she is travelling abroad: the train "whistled shrilly as Lisbon swept past / and everywhere I looked, my eyes deceived me. / . . . I knew you / had gone. Your ghost flew past." Then the ominous observation, "The Station clock said 7:16 when I arrived, the train / on time, even here . . . ," while she is supposed to be vacationing: "wind burning my face, summer headlong toward me / and nothing to hold onto but your death." A profoundly moving lament.

In the poem that places second, "The Origins of the Kiss," Patricia Young explores what we generally take to be an attribute of physical love. Longing and desire are the pivotal emotions here, and the way the poet plays with the human urge to 'taste' the environment is both humorous and touching. Beside its more light-hearted connotation, the poet alludes to the biting and sucking aspect of the kiss, and then, on an even more sinister level, there is the "great, / unlit kiss that feeds on mud at the bottom/ of the lake — that ancient and primitive / longing" that we know almost from the day we were born.

Gabriele Guenther's third-ranked poem "Oil of Fear" describes a relationship between the two young children of different cultural backgrounds, that might have unfolded and blossomed, but in fact folded in upon itself and collapsed, "heavy as a dead / body, or a religion / prying apart our folded hands."

The fact that the girl realizes she will "be spared / the furor / rampant between two separate / worlds" does little to soothe our fears for the future of either of these worlds.

The three prize winners in 1993 were all women. I have no particular wish to right the balance, but I will mention a few poems by men here, because they especially caught my eye and ear: David Manicom's "Radiation" leaves both cadences and images that reverberate and settle in the bone; Samuel Peralta's "A Mother" amazes with a child's crystal-clear view of his parents; John Unrau, in "The Goodlooking Newsreader on Channel X" lightens the mood, imagining a boring newscaster as the prophet of a hidden god.

Singling out Susan McMaster's "The Gardener's Dream" with its careful pleats and meticulous stitches as a delightful bit of fantasy could easily set me on the road to assembling many other triads of poems worth mentioning. But the entire collection deserves close attention. For me, reading this book is like looking at the crown of the tree I've looked up to for so long, only this time from above, seeing the glossy surface of the leaves and the brilliant blooms the branches and twigs have brought forth. I am grateful to the contributors, both League members and others, for providing a bouquet as vibrant as this.

Maria Jacobs
Toronto, March 1994

Notes on the Authors

TIM BOWLING, a native of Vancouver, has had poems published in various journals, including *Capilano Review, Grain, Event, Queen's Quarterly* and *Poetry Canada.* He is presently compiling his first collection of work. He writes, "Awards? Let's just say the Governor General's banker isn't losing any sleep over me. Besides, a bark of approval from my black lab, MacKenzie King, is reward enough."

DENISE CAMMIADE is involved in the book trade, and books and gardens seem to be prominent passions, at present. Occasionally she finds time to scribble the odd line. She has been published in *The Malahat Review*. If she got it together to send out poems more often, perhaps she would be published elsewhere, too!

RON CHARACH is a practising psychiatrist, living in Toronto. His second collection of poems, *Someone Else's Memoirs*, was published by Quarry in 1994. He recently edited *The Naked Physician, Poems about the Lives of Patients and Doctors* (Quarry, 1990).

MÉIRA COOK is a graduate student at the University of Manitoba. Her first book of poetry, *A Fine Grammar of Bones*, was published by Turnstone in 1993, and a chapbook, *String Quartet*, will be published by disOrientations (Alberta) in 1994.

WILLIAM (BILL) FLEDDERUS is a journalist now pursuing a Master of Arts in creative writing at the University of Alberta. Previously he studied under author-professor Hugh Cook at Redeemer College in Ancaster, Ontario.

WAYNE GABRIEL lives at the mouth of the Rouge River with his wife and three children. His work has been published in *White Wall Review, The Amethyst Review*, and *Surface and Symbol.*

ANN GOLDRING is the author of "Old Matt," one of the top nineteen short stories in a national contest, and published in *The Blue Jean Collection* (Thistledown, 1992). She teaches Language Arts at an adult secondary school and is an active participant in writing for children workshops at George Brown College.

SUSAN GOYETTE is originally from Montreal. She now lives in Dartmouth, Nova Scotia where she is working on her first manuscript of poems. Her poetry has appeared in *TickleAce*, and will be in an upcoming edition of *Fiddlehead*.

NEILE GRAHAM is a Canadian writer currently living in Seattle, Washington. Her work has been published in American and Canadian magazines, in *More Garden Varieties Two* (Mercury, 1990), and in the collection, *Seven Robins* (Penumbra, 1983).

MARIE GROUNDWATER was born in the Orkney Islands, Scotland, and emigrated to Canada as a child. A teacher in Windsor, Ontario, she has had writing published at the University of Windsor, in *Generation 90*, and the *Grand Wayzgoose Anthologies*.

GABRIELE GUENTHER is Third Prize winner of the League of Canadian Poets 1993 National Poetry Contest. She is a Toronto poet currently working for Deutsche Welle TV in Germany. Her work has appeared in such journals as *ARC*, *Dandelion*, *Quarry Magazine* and *Vintage 92* (Sono Nis, 1992).

LALA HEINE-KOEHN was born in Poland and emigrated to Saskatchewan where she began to paint and write poetry. She writes, "At one time someone said I have one lover only: the sun. I am not that virtuous. I have two: the sun and poetry and I am always fearful of their betrayal."

GARY HYLAND is a high school English teacher and editor, living in Moose Jaw, Saskatchewan. He recently won the Saskatchewan Writers' Guild poetry manuscript contest for his book, *After Atlantis* (Thistledown, 1992).

JOY KIRSTIN is the First Prize winner of the League of Canadian Poets 1993 National Poetry Contest. She lives in Victoria, British Columbia, where she enjoys sailing, practises magic, and earns her living as a writer. She has lived and travelled extensively in Europe and the former Soviet Union, and spent a year hitchhiking alone through Africa. She describes herself as the laziest poet she knows.

Zoë Landale is a winner of the 1992 *Event* Creative Non-Fiction Competition, the 1992 Canadian Church Press best narrative and the 1993 Stony Brook University (New York) Short Fiction Competition. She has had two books of poetry published, *Harvest of Salmon* (Hancock House, 1977) and *Colour of Winter Air* (Sono Nis, 1991).

Annette LeBox lives in Maple Ridge, British Columbia. She is enrolled in the MFA programme in creative writing at the University of British Columbia. She has completed a collection of poems, *the absence of flowers*, and is currently working on a children's novel.

John B. Lee, author of fifteen books, was named the 1993 winner of the Milton Acorn Memorial People's Poetry Award, and placed second in the poetry section of the 1991 CBC Literary Competition. He has published a number of books of poetry.

David Manicom is a Foreign Service Officer with the Canadian Embassy in Moscow. He has a PhD in English Literature from McGill University and has published short fiction, academic articles, and reviews in Canada, the U.S. and Ireland.

Karen Massey has been living and working in Ottawa for the past three years. She received her MA in English (Creative Writing) from Concordia University in Montreal in 1992, with a thesis on poetry.

Nadine McInnis is the author of, *Shaking the Dreamland Tree* (Coteau, 1986), *The Litmus Body* (Quarry, 1992), which received the Ottawa-Carleton 1993 Book Award, and the forthcoming *The Poetry of Desire: A Critical Study of Dorothy Livesay* (Turnstone, 1994). She was First Prize winner of the 1992 League of Canadian Poets National Poetry Contest and placed second in the poetry section of the 1993 CBC Literary Competition.

Susan McMaster is an Ottawa poet whose books and tapes include poetry, theatre scripts and collaborative wordmusic scores with the intermedia group First Draft. *The Hummingbird Murders* (Quarry, 1992) and *Learning to Ride* (Quarry, 1994) are her most recent books.

SHARON H. NELSON's recent books include *The Work of Our Hands* (Muses' Company, 1992), which was short listed for the A.M. Klein Poetry Prize, *Grasping Men's Metaphors* (Muses', 1993) and *Family Scandals* (Muses', Spring 1994). She served as founding co-ordinator of the Feminist Caucus of the League of Canadian Poets and was founding CEO of the Federation of English-language Writers of Quebec.

SANDRA NICHOLLS' first book, *The Untidy Bride* (Quarry, 1991) was short-listed for the 1991 Pat Lowther Award from the League of Canadian Poets. Her poems and short stories have appeared in literary magazines across Canada, including *Dandelion*, *Grain*, *The Antigonish Review*, and *Room of One's Own.* Her work has been anthologized in two collections and broadcast on CBC radio. She currently teaches part-time at St. Francis Xavier University in Antigonish, Nova Scotia.

BARBARA COLEBROOK PEACE has worked for some years in art galleries, and is now taking a year off to write poetry. She is working on her first book of poems, *Underworld: First Winter*. Her poems have been published in *The Windhorse Review* and *The Gulf Island Guardian*.

SAMUEL B. PERALTA is a poet and physicist. His honours include the Palanca Award for Literature in his native Philippines, and awards from the BBC and the U.K. Poetry Society. He lives quietly near Toronto with his wife Alice and one inscrutable tabby cat.

MATTHEW REMSKI's poems have appeared in journals across the continent. Two collections, *Canticles for a Fifth Season* and *The Centrifugal Heart,* are forthcoming from Guernica. He was named co-winner of the 1993 Malahat Long Poem Contest. He lives in Toronto, where he studies and is employed as a church organist.

FAYE SCOTT RIEGER is the finest feminist tapdancer and writer. She has been a top finalist in many poetry and fiction contests, and has published widely in both Canada and the U.S. Two of her recent short stories are in *Matrix* and *White Wall Review*.

LINDA ROGERS is a performance poet who is famous for her bread. She and her husband write and perform songs for children. Her awards include the 1990 B.C. Writers Poetry Prize. Her latest book *The Magic Flute* (Porcupine's Quill, 1991) won an Alcuin award.

Ron Smith lives in Lantzville, British Columbia, teaches at Malaspina College in Nanaimo, and is publisher of Oolichan Books. His stories and poems have appeared in magazines and anthologies in Canada, England, Australia and Yugoslavia. His books include *Seasonal* and *A Buddha Named Baudelaire*.

Elyse Yates St. George lives in Saskatoon, Saskatchewan. Her work has appeared in art and literary publications. Her first book of poetry and art, *White Lions in the Afternoon*, was published by Coteau in 1989. She is currently working on a new poetry manuscript and an exhibition of paintings to be mounted at the Mendel Art Gallery in Saskatoon in 1995.

Carmine Starnino lives in Montreal, where he is completing an honours degree in English and Creative Writing at Condordia University. In 1991 he received the Irving Layton Creative Writing Award for Poetry. His poems are forthcoming in *Quarry*, and *Poetry Canada Review*, and he currently serves as poetry editor for *errata*, the Montreal arts magazine.

Anna Synenko has had poetry published in *Grain*, *Prism International* and *Room of One's Own*. She is presently working on a short story collection, *Whole Cloth*.

John Unrau started writing poetry about five years ago and has had poems published in *Garden Varieties* (Cormorant, 1988) and *More Garden Varieties* (Mercury, 1989), anthologies of the top fifty poems of previous League of Canadian Poets National Poetry Contests.

Patricia Young is the winner of Second Prize in the 1993 League of Canadian Poets National Poetry Contest. She has had four books of poetry published and has received numerous awards for her poetry. Her most recent book, *More Watery Still* (House of Anansi, 1992), was nominated for the 1992 Governor General's Award for Poetry.

Vintage 93

League of Canadian Poets

Gabriele Guenther

Oil of Fear

Far from the half-timbered flanks
of the school-house, the ocean
a mute gray mouth at our feet,
we'd spend recess, perched
high above the playground,
body parts dangling lopsided
as paper cranes from the brick wall, my
young lips working
loose wonders around your oblong Persian
vowels that you'd bring me daily
sculpted into something like a special lunch.
You already knew how to read then,
glazing my palms with the cup-like stems
of those words. And you knew all about the darkness
prowling angry in men

who made splits, as you called it,
of women's legs.
I'd just learned the sleeved
loops of tongue that meant my name
was close enough
to be touched open
by a new intricate script, the dots
like puzzles of saliva
milky as your laugh.

We were nine that year, in fourth grade,
and our thighs the same size, though
later we grew to be ashamed
of our difference, heavy as a dead
body, or a religion
prying apart our folded hands.

When we were seventeen, and estranged,
you'd come into French class
draped in the stiff black
mask of your grandmother's blood
on letters that demanded you
return immediately
to Iran to marry. All that year
I watched that *prospective husband*
gathering like a ruche at your neck
and wrist. Knowing that, after graduation,
I'd be the one who would be spared
the furor
rampant between two separate
worlds. A split thin red
laugh would soon tunnel together, and polish
to rock with the oil of fear.

Hope

I am the nurse assigned
to manipulate her limbs.
A woman in my arms, docile,
smooth as wax, given over
to my will to move
her.

Each day she grows lighter.
I unhook her fluids
from over her head,
bags yield warm in my hands,
her pregnant belly
translucent
rises like a bubble.

sometimes it's more
like rocking a baby
to the moody mid-afternoon
transmissions of the hospital
than any partnership
between consenting
adults.

Is this what men want most?

Men in parliament, men
with their heads
inclined together, their whispers
hardening into laws.

Polka music, rag-time, hard cruel
rock, I've tried them all,
but nothing moves her
through this marathon
we've embarked on
together, her feet shifting
slightly by my urgings,
a woman
dancing unconscious in my arms.

Now I've begun to imagine
I dance with the child
growing inside her.
Don't give up hope,
the men in the board
rooms scold.

No, I don't know the woman's
name. Let her be *Hope*,
and I'm giving her up.

The child seeing
through her dissolving skin
my white uniform,
feels me rocking him
like a guardian angel,

mistakes me, perhaps for her,
a ghostly vision
of the guide his mother
has moved far beyond
dancing them both, gently,
on their way.

Nadine McInnis

Swimming Lesson

My daughter has been chosen
to drown.
She flails her arms, slipping
and rising out of the foam she's created
with her usual grace.

She drowns so prettily
all the mothers in the balcony
smile down on her, then turn back
to their toddlers, aimless conversations
slowed by vapours rising
from the overheated pool.

Even I am amused
by the way she surrenders herself,
and the playful calls from the edge:
"Hold on." "Are you in trouble?"
do nothing to change
her elaborate dance with fate.

Until the young man
with lean muscles and perfect strokes
throws her a life-ring,
lies flat on the deck,
reaches with his eager sure hand.
"Kick! C'mon, swim to me."
and across a choppy yard of chlorinated water
their hands move closer together,
then join.

Soon, he'll be demonstrating
something new,
easing her down, tipping back her chin
with a soft nudge of his hand,
his mouth close to her mouth,
pausing, listening for her heart.

Nadine McInnis

Walking on Water

We walked on water
to the lighthouse anchored in the channel
past Duck Island, that thin strip of trees,
unpopulated. Only the illusion of land,
a web of tree-roots snaking down
into the dingy river that moved on endlessly
while we tossed in our sleep.

We never set foot there in summer.
Only in winter were we drawn out onto the ice
where a distant blue light swung and blinded
like a migraine, like our intense longing
to move on. Hazy with desire,
that cloud of fish-flies disorienting us,
as we trudged along shore, then inched out
onto the creaky ice towards the lighthouse
where you carved my name.

Spring nights we lay
together in your parents' basement
the river rising in the dark, voluptuous
lapping that washed our dull neighbourhood
of its omissions, train whistles far off
hurting us less in that moment,
the moan of massive shadows, imagined
as ships that moved along the river only at night,
ships we would board separately
as stowaways. You first, then me.
I looked forward to not knowing one day
where you might be.

Today I walk the shore with my children
calling them back from the allure
of the edge. For now, casting stones
is enough. They haven't looked out to where
only the concrete base of the lighthouse remains.
My name is gone. That little permanence
we risked our lives for,
swept into a black current.

A miracle, this growing up, knowing now
what the danger is called: *candle ice*,
walking on *candle ice*, pale columns
cold as wax, tunnels we might have slipped down,
flaming only with one moment's
wish, to vanish without leaving a trace.

JOHN UNRAU

The Goodlooking Newsreader on Channel X

In ancient Didyma
Apollo's priestess sat
bathing feet and sacred robe
in the mystic spring
till vapour rising from her perfumed hem
filled her with the power of the god
and all the grove with cries and mutterings.

The prophet meanwhile standing by
would turn her gibberish into verse.
Most days he had it all prepared
before the Mystery commenced,
but it was boring hackwork and sometimes
he'd start the session with the crazy hope
that something in the way she mouthed and moaned
might stir him past his sleepy formulas.

I often think of him while hearing you
reading in your nasal high-pitched twang
the latest news of local happenings.
With all my other muses gone on leave
I turn to you night after dreary night
through all your shifts in makeup, clothes and hair
and shutting off the sound imagine you
murmuring in pentecostal tongues
the teleprompting s of some hidden god.

Ron Smith

Fires of Chernobyl

1

April 26, 1986

As we watch the news, my son and I see
you plunge into the blaze. We are puzzled

by the spade you hold in your hands. Who are you?
A blood-red sun explodes in the tortured sky.

The house of cards that carries you to your death
is falling down. Say it will die with you.

Say that the graphite debris you shovel
down into the sarcophagus feeds

the political will; that the State
leaves you to your solitude, to enjoy

the last threads of light before you are collected
into darkness, into a forest of crosses.

Say others care as I do for your sacrifice.
Say your act is embedded in our minds

as is our love for rivers, clear air and growing things.
Say that in going into the inferno, into the dead zone

invisible as it was, you have healed my mind
and closed the wound. Wine for an endless thirst.

I will sing for you. My garden is green
and my voice strong. When your body is taken

and laid in the ground, may your spirit live here
and others find it green and growing and abundant.

May your children feel at home in our place.
May they know that wherever they go in their dreams

they walk on their father's ashes, their
father's burned and poisoned flesh. Their father's love

As we bend to harvest, to turn the dark earth,
we learn to walk softly on sacred ground.

2

Five years later, Dr. Chernousenko, physicist, reveals
officials ordered him to "liquidate the consequences."

This is the power of murderers. The magic
to turn light into darkness, energy to mass:

to reverse equations, invite apocalypse.
To set men on fire, blind to what they would destroy.

My son says he finally understands. He can see
through the wall of words. He can feel the torment

of the men who danced the minute waltz
on the rooftop, their eyes extinguished like coals,

their dragons never to be slain by the sword.
For thirty kilometres, the country they love is haunted

by the ghosts of fields and forests and villages.
35 million people damaged, Mr. Chernousenko says.

Beyond boundaries, death rides the winds and a child
traces shapes of imaginary beasts in faraway clouds.

Ron Smith

Partners

October 26, 1992

The two men fighting in the street begin
from habit. Confirm the invisible.
The same brown bag rests against the wall
where each has pissed away his emptiness;

where each has reconstructed history,
built stories from razed and burning towns.
They spin and shuffle in the winter rain
return to the feeble dance that swirls

in their brains, a madcap moment
where yesterday is always absent.
They are partners who swing at each other;
lovers whose lips cut on the end of a fist.

Each desires to speak of love but this word
lives in a distant moment of their lives.
The one convulses at the thought, draws a knife,
a new twist added by the tilting scale of night.

The blade rips into the other's belly.
A deep wound. When did they begin to feud?
Their private war scatters pigeons into
an empty sky. Shadows lurk behind the eye

and the torn man feels the cold push up
into his heart. This country is muted.
The man with the knife in his hand steps back,
stares at the figure lying in the street.

The scene before him is another story;
the corpse belongs to someone else's indignation.
The smoke of an alley fire chokes his cries
and he flings his arms and body back

against the wall and fears to close his eyes
on the one who has abandoned him.

Matthew Remski

Dying in the Family

> *All my people are larger bodies than mine,*
> *quiet, with voices gentle and meaningless*
> *like the voices of sleeping birds. . . . One is*
> *my mother who is good to me. One is my*
> *father who is good to me.*
>
> —James Agee,
> A Death in the Family

The January night, the restless universe.

The choices become important in the hours between daylight.

This is what happens when God
becomes a myth looking for a family.
He will not seek you at midday.
He will not seek you beside cold mountain streams.
He will seek you when you sit beside yourself,
calling the bones by name.

Woman, you are sleeping because you know this.
Aren't we all afraid?

I would talk to you about children,
but every child on the planet is dead.

I would talk to you about parents,
but they are gone as well.

We have the sun, and the unexpected friend, sure.
But nothing like the doors of the world
flying open to a grove of children.
Nothing like the parents, spreading quilts.

This is worse than we can talk about,
the thudding heart, the blood making a wrong turn.

There are no summer evenings anymore.
This is worse than the weatherman forecasting
the next birthday.

Come and go, come and go.
Eating good american soil to our deaths.
Giving each other a brief peace at every pass.

Brief and insubstantial, punctuated by trolleys,
and the filaments that leave us behind.

O James, o James, what is the moon,
and how are the tides of the heart made livable?

Little Boy with Hands Up

(a Holocaust photo)

Dear little boy in a Warsaw cap
holding back tears, with your hands up,
heart-breaking knees so naked
between shorts and knee-high socks
under a coat you're growing out of,

caught like a mouse
in an adult trap.

Mother walks beside you
but is too far away, for that,
distracted from your care, checking
to see if They're getting ready to shoot,
if maybe They're about to shoot,

your sister, next to *Baba*
somewhere far behind
though in the same photo!
they too hold their hands in the air
for the Nazi bogey men.

The far right corner gives us a good look at two of them,
one, highly professional, holding an automatic,
though noticing
your mother's long and pretty hair.
In years to come
any number of actors will play them, with accents,
Kirk Douglas and Karl Malden
for these two —

But how to play your Father,
his eye barely visible behind *Baba*'s raised arm
as he looks straight ahead into space —

into the space of a vacated ghetto,
all worldly possessions abandoned
according to Luther's plan,
Hitler's decree.

There are other young boys in line,
and another father in a cap,
and a hand held up in the background
looks more like it's waving
than surrendering —

Dear little boy, in an indented cap,
though you mustn't look behind you now,
someone older, who would love you,
is waving Goodbye!

The Dead Rise in Us

The dead rise in us
fragrant as pine
& green with needles of stories
they never did get figured out.

It is up to us
to finish them.
The dead wait, anxious as children at bed-time,
to see how their stories will turn out this time.

They don't tell us, though, that our narratives
grow rooted from theirs, or can't,
in that thin eyeblink universe away
from flesh.

Time means nothing to the dead.
Rectifying does,
emotions which batter the living, still,
knotted lies we mistake for our own.

The sheer bright energy
the dead wasted thinking themselves
animals in cold houses
they laboured endlessly to warm.

Suffering.

So they give the luminous tail-ends of hurt
to us. Red columbines flowering
Fifteen hundred feet above a mountain lake,
red columbines flower
rasp of breath as we pull ourselves higher.

Not that the dead focus upon us,
they are somewhere between air
sweet from that lake
& the pinwheel of fresh-minted galaxies,

Resolving whatever problems the fleshless encounter.
Hoping that this time, the stories come out
undistorted.
Theirs. Ours. Clear wood.

Solving the stories. Absolving.
Pine in the sunshine, the gusts we have of *knowing*
when we let the dead speak.
Our grandfathers died despising their failings —

An insight which lifts us practically off the path
as we bite down hard on feeling we had thought ours.
Clues.
There is a right shape to be here,

One not made with hands.
As if our kindness reaches backward
& touches them. As one day descendants
may comfort us.

Lupines, still blooming at high elevations
their glorious blue
the colour of forgiveness,
of stories growing clear.

Sharon H. Nelson

Portrait of a Lady

The soil warms through long afternoons and cools at night.
"This June has been too cool for basil or early flowering of roses."
The tulips lost their heads, as usual, to early heat, but that has passed.
We had a dry spring, and then this long coolness, humidity in the air, wetness of earth.
"Our seasons, like our weather lately, seem remarkable."

We are people who speak of gardens, the shoots of tender growth,
the particular, Latin names of plants. We are people with an eye on the sky,
concerned with weather, the rate that water falls, the textures of the earth,
its insufficiencies, its separate parts: clay, sand, humus, compost, peat.
We make our beds meticulously, careful as a surgical nurse.

The late night air is cool. A Beethoven concerto drifts
across my consciousness, fills the interstices between my thoughts
as if a garden fork had shifted earth, aerating it.
Now I have worms on the brain, "a sign of life," my neighbour says.

A clever wife, she nurses children, husband, plants, and keeps her silences,
and feels the earth in her small plot, and walks her dog and runs with it enough
for its good health, and watches where the earth worms trek, following with her eyes
where worms abide. She is a woman who never says what she thinks,
but her hands scratch at the dry earth, cool or warm, with a desperation that speaks.

We have discussed columbine, the growth of weeds.
She never tans; her garden's mostly in the shade,
but as her skin tautens on her face,
her eyes fade. She does not speak of this or anything
besides the growth of flowers, condition of the soil, local weather.
Whatever grief is in her moves, like worms, within the compost of her heart
where it is always quiet, cool, and dark.

A Mother

Next year, we promised ourselves,
we'd have to get it for her next year,
that sculpture in cork and ivory:
framed in a world of glass,
a house smaller than her thumbnail
and trees and reeds
and a bridge to an island
where miniature cranes spread their wings
for flight.

When she saw it first, a month ago,
at that shop in Ayala,
she held it up to the light
with both hands.
She was so afraid it would slip!

Her dreams were larger
than our twelve-year-old pockets.
Instead, papa helped us wrap up
a china cat we'd found
in a sea front store.
We hid it under the towels
in the closet.

That afternoon we put on records
and papa did impressions
with a made-up guitar.
Then there was that smoky, rich, funny
smell coming from the oven . . .
We looked at each other, then raced
to the kitchen in twos.
She laughed, and he laughed too,
as she scraped
the burnt-out bottom of his coffee cake
from the pan.
We didn't.

After dinner we gathered around her,
our hearts beating
like so many small wings.
First the white ribbon, then the box,
then the layered tissues.
"Oh!" she said. "Oh!"
and she held it to her cheek.

There between the lamplight
and the window, rocked in his arms,
she held it to her cheek.

Concatenations

Can we find a place where we can meet
not in silence, not in sound?"

— Children of a Lesser God

You taught me to lip read Bach, placing
my hands on his mouth as he sang. He was
like standing by the sea, feeling the sound
of the earth tremor and the hidden voice
of the coral in my bones.

Listen — in this concatenation of silences
there is something I want for you to hear,
for all the dreams you made my own, for longing,
for pain, for all you are. I want to say — there,
in my throat, the words catch like salt.

I am trying to say your name,
the semaphore that brings you to me.
Fingers joined in two circles mean *to connect.*
When I move them thus, it is *to join*.
I am coming out of the silence.

Read my lips. Watch my hands. Translate
my heart from that Rosetta stone
embedded in your soul. This —
this is the sign for *need*, and this
the sign for *you*, and this — is *stay*.

Savannah

A current crosses the darkness,
stirring the last dry shreds of life.

Upwind, a Buick stalks the edge of the pavement,
its voice a gentle rumble in its throat.

Its eyes simmer like the smoke snarling up
from a hammered anvil.

The neon tattoos its skin so it is
striped orange, a strobed tiger, crouched, impatient.

Feather and ivory. A slow, livid burning
in the undergrowth.

Just under the awnings they flash phosphorescence
flamingo flamingo and then vanish into air.

From the antlered shadows a drunkard lurches.
His legs spindle under him like a newborn gazelle.

The window blinds drift and flutter,
hovering wings.

Somewhere on the savannah something watches
with incandescent eyes.

Arrival

alone by his desk at night
he tracks the movements of turtles
gliding through water, their scarred
leather shells paint olive shadows
across the dark floor of the Atlantic,
soft green flippers in languid prayer
as they swim hundreds of miles
in a world of quiet, scarcely able to hear

where do they come from?
where do they go?

weightless beneath the surface
their huge sea bodies,
filled with eggs, move blindly,
pulled to land
by the strange sounding
of old mating grounds,
yet they are no more than blips
on his screen
black dots that pulse slowly
across the single dimension
of a computerized map
moon, tide, weather,
what brings them here?
what underwater code
is kept secret from him,
he waits for *arribada*, the arrival
of the turtles, for the tears to stream
from dark, mournful eyes
as they lay their eggs
in the soft, deep sand
and crawl back to the sea,
it's an old mystery
and he wants it explained

where do they come from?
where do they go?

night turns to early morning
he drowses over a cup of cold coffee
in the lab, while under the sea
the turtles move in strange waves
confused by the lure of satellites
poised in deep space
and the signals which seem
to hum beneath their skin,
he fails to observe
thousands of miles away
hundreds of turtles
like huge boulders pushing
through the surface of the sea
and swimming madly
for the sky.

Crash Test Dummies

"When is the baby due?" one man
asks another. "They don't seem to know,"
he replies, shuffling back and forth
"doctor says it's her blood pressure,"
they both look away,
their dark heads frosted
with new-falling snow,
and stare into a window
of toys on display,
the year's best seller for Christmas:
The Incredible Crash Test Dummies
complete with crumpling hood
and warnings to buckle up,
they even have names:
Slick, Axel, and Skid the Kid.

Settled into his car, he remembers
first time behind the wheel, his father
saying "don't tell your mother,
she'll worry," as if women could somehow
be protected from worry,
he remembers his father explaining
the fluids and pressures of a '68 Valiant,
while tonight, his wife at home
watches the snow as the baby shifts
under her skin, she is learning
how to worry, for the unborn
for the night, and strangers in cars,
for the first time your children walk away
and don't turn back,
until finally a click at the door
her husband shakes the sparks
of snow from his hair,

the cat rushes past their feet
into the blizzard, disappears
he calls to the cat, but his voice
lost in the wind, disappears
and later as he presses his ear
to his wife's belly, he tries not to show
his fear, and the image he worries she might see
playing over and over again across his eyes:
the soft bodies coming apart
in slow motion, the slamming together
of brick and steel, the bodies flung forward, helpless,
headfirst, their limbs in pieces, and the smiles painted
on their sailing, wooden faces.

Sandra Nicholls

Whales

At night the whales appear
from underwater caves
or pushing upwards through the floor,
she drives back their snub-nosed armies
with forks and knives,
weapons too small for the size
of the enemy, but at least they feel
familiar in her hands. She has chosen
carefully the most delicate weapons
she can find.

Barely surfaced from the green-blue
ocean of blankets, she lies in bed,
unable to move, watching her husband,
while the dream echoes in the dark,
half-awake, she struggles to interpret
he stops her mid-sentence:
she should get out and exercise more.
He doesn't understand
it's dangerous work
spending the days alone
imagining the invisible
children they didn't have,
for now the timing's off,
the singing in her body gone.

The whales come in daylight now,
she barely needs to close her eyes
to see them, but she misses the others,
the ones who used to visit
in the afternoons, small, tender,
whispering from bedroom walls,
the children in hiding, waiting
their turn, afraid of the whales,
afraid to come out.

Man Watching His Sarongs Dry

The pale-skinned man
in the grass hut has six sarongs.
I have counted them.
He hangs them out to dry,
watches them rise like spirits
from the dead, their diaphanous
skirts floating on the sea air.

He winds these sheets
about his limbs, his body
turning as a hand keeping
the day's time. He wears
one sarong then another
as if he is a polygamous
husband wanting to please.

But maybe I have imagined this;
perhaps his torso is a wound and
the gauze, the colour of pallid tangerines
and mangoes, a healing cloth.
Perhaps he changes his dressing
according to the slant of light,
bilious sunset, gangrenous dawn.

The man watches his sarongs dry.
The colours bleed; the cloth
grows thinner. He folds
his sarongs as a miser
piles gold, the coins tumbling
through his fingers, imprinting
their faces into his skin.

If the sarongs are his mantra,
then the folds must be disillusionment,
the colours, joy, and the threads, repentance.
I am trying to solve this; the thrill of the cloth
beneath his fingers, the tenderness of his imaginings
as the lengths soar in the wind's gibberish.
The secrets of these incantations.

The Certain Days of Abstinence

Today began the certain days of the Fifth Month
of Abstinence. No flowery clothes, no flowery
thoughts and I am wearing again the robe,
still mossy from gloom of other such days.
The yuku shell on the lacquered tray is empty
of wine, looks as desolate as I. For it is
an ill-spent time not to be held or touched,
not even glanced at by anyone.

I try to discipline myself, accept this bondage,
passed on by sages shrivelled husks, too old
for all pleasure even when first born.
I kneel on the straw mat, disk reappears
at appointed time, padding all corners with darkness.
I strain to look through the heavy folds of kicho,
at the magnificent embroidery depicting the ancient,
venerated rituals that extol meditation and pious
prayers. Alas, I crave food, drink, a reckless
lover who abides no deity or master.
Somewhere, from under the veranda step, a sound,
as if a whimper of a child, stirs the static air,
a cat must be giving birth to a litter.

25.V. – 15.VI.92

Cleopatra's Ring

In the changing rooms of desire
women gossip, their eyes
at eye level,
holding their stomach in.
They shower and talk about
children and books.
This one's daughter is dead,
her grandson waiting outside
near the coke machine
with incorrect change.
That one swims in her jewels,
I tell her she might go under
like the Duchess of Windsor,
her exiled emeralds plodding
across the Atlantic,
the little prince beside her,
wearing his Anglican waterwings,
saying over and over, mama,
mama, as if she could save him now.
In the locker room, the men
talk about women and politics,
measure each other's penises.
Their wives read tabloids.
They all desire Diana,
her lovely long legs and real tiara.
Someone remembers hearing
the former Prince of Wales
had a tiny plume
for writing, but never mind.
His Duchess learned about love
in a Hong Kong singing house.
He says the Duchess had Cleopatra's ring.
It's a muscle, you know, like Mitzi
the table dancer who played
flute with her vagina.

That one who rises
and sinks in her jewels is amazed
I can cross the pool on my back
without moving my arms and legs.
I tell her my grandmother also
danced with the Prince of Wales.

Maybe I Like To Sing

Maybe I like to sing
because of the sister
they scraped from my father's
girlfriend's womb
in an abortionist's kitchen,
the table sticky with jam and coffee
and other women's blood,
the radio turned up
to cover her screams.
Maybe it played Paper Doll,
my parents' favourite song.
Maybe my sister wanted to be
a country and western singer
in cowboy boots and fringy skirts
in saloons with chicken wire over the stage
in case the customers wanted to grope
or throw their bottles and flickering smokes
at her half-Italian thighs.
Maybe she wanted to be a diva.
I was born knowing the words
to Italian art songs.
She must have learned them first
while her mother played roulette with her fingers,
my father and the grand piano
squeezed in the back of her father's store.
Her father was a poor immigrant
and my grandmother danced with the Prince of Wales.
My father chose, but not me.
After my sister fell
limp in a metal bowl,
he gave my mother quinine
and a diamond ring
and told her to throw herself
down the stairs.

But, warned by my sister,
I was awake and listening
and dug my long fingernails,
and aristocratic prerogative,
into her womb as my mother
fell like a circus acrobat,
into his net.

Palindrome

The door to my son's room is shut.
Inside, it might be snowing.
A fine dust settles
on Tristan and his brothers.
If I were allowed inside,
I might see them as they would look
after I am dead,
their hair and eyebrows chalky,
their flexible backs
bent into question marks,
the way Tristan folded himself
like a paper flame
into my skirt that night in Seattle
when his nose bled through the last act
of an opera by Wagner.
"I want to see Valhalla burn," he said then,
"put my hands on the hot drawbridge
and feel it singing."
His bedroom door is cold to the touch.
I stand outside and bargain and plead,
"I made a cake. Your noses will bleed."
I hear it snowing in there
and Keefer reciting
an old book from back to front.
"Dogma: I am god is dogma: I am god spelled backwards.",
he reads, and I understand I am hearing
the frantic chisel of Michelangelo
releasing the incoherent
voices of prophets from marble.
My sons eat cheese and have psychedelic dreams.
They wear their sweaters inside out,
and watch the news on television.
While a mad king burns in Windsor Chapel
and Yugoslav brides in satin dresses
scour the rubble of war
for their missing arms and legs,

my children send notes under Tristan's door.
"Lepers repel is lepers repel spelled backwards."
I believe I'm being punished now
for the time I lied about Christmas
to boys who see numbers reversed
and read in tongues like Michelangelo's
prophets trapped in the rock.
I will stand on my head and knock
until the door has twenty-five windows.
Then I'll open them one by one and discover
love in a room full of birds flying upside down,
my children's hands hammering and filing,
freeing them from stone.

Remember the Child

Someone has boarded the mission,
nailed in the sound of an Inuit
altar boy crying in the dark,
his bottom bleeding.
Remember the child
they found frozen in his pyjamas
the morning after he ran away.

This child watched his father
carve the soapstone
you showed me, two polar bears,
one on the other —
six feet on the ground,
his breast rubbing the happy
arch of her spine,
his face grinning into the arctic sun,
the white sound of their pleasure
louder than organ music in church.

You said the carver
put down his knife on holy days
and entered his wife
smiling like a man
who knows how a blade
melts into rock.
You said he tithed with stone,
married his woman in church
and gave their child to the priest.

You said the priest
accepted the carver's gift
and the carver's child for God, then
cut off the bear's head and arms
and smoothed the dam's elongated back.

You said he kept his head low
as he entered the boy
and disappeared like sugar in tea
until they were also an animal with six legs.

LINDA ROGERS

Smells Around the Mouth

In the wild, they say,
animals lick their young
to get rid of the smell
and protect them from predators.
They say, some animals are born
formless and shaped by their mothers' tongues.
In some families in my neighbourhood,
a licking meant your mother
took a wooden spoon
and bent you over a kitchen chair,
your bum exposed, then she would say:
"I'm licking you into shape."
My mother didn't own a spoon like that,
but she did tell us the stories of girls
who forgot to cover their smells,
how the odour of cigarettes and sex
could ruin your life.
She warned us about ice-cream and lipstick.
Mother said smells around the mouth
attracted stinging insects.
We knew she meant men
when she licked her cotton
handkerchief and wiped our faces.
My sister and I still remember
the frightened taste of her breath
and how we slowly began to look like her.

The Photograph

for my mother

Uncherished in the family catalogue,
found creased, yellow-edged,
at the bottom of a shoe box
stuffed in a cupboard,
it speaks to me more than
all the others, more than
my flesh, and in a voice
I almost recognize, soft
and far away

Yet the scene itself is common
to those years:

in my sister's infant hand
a strawberry ice-cream cone blazes
like a torch, lighting up,
along the lily-pad float,
my father and teenaged brothers
shirtless in the April sun,
their bodies slim and pale
as three long cigarettes
as they pose, grinning,
beside a dead chinook salmon,
sixty-plus pounds, held under the gills
by my father's strong, invisible grip:
beyond, the river is full of life
swimming towards a single purpose
high in the distant valley;
its calm is the calm
of chemicals in a darkroom sink,
poised for transformation,
the magic leap of images
drawn from nothing to the light

It's taken me years to understand
why their happiness pains me:
youth cannot accommodate absence;
the woman's shadow on the mossy planks,
her thumb in the corner of the frame,
the date she's written on the back
in a still-shaky hand
months after their loss:
its taken me years to realize
the truest photographs never appear

Soon, the pose dissolves,
the ice-cream melts down my sister's hand
in trickles, like the chinook's blood
along its scales; the taut muscle
of my father's arm slackens,
his strong sons laugh,
and the tiny shadow within the shadow
turns naturally to the sound,
the salt of life already sweet
upon its mouth,
each perfect crystal another word
waiting to be voiced;
while the greater shadow,
river-still,
follows its own dark purpose
out of the frame

Somewhere in a valley grave he's buried
the one who took the bear's paw in his flesh
that I might surface to the sun,
the one who thrashed upon the tides of blood
that I might reach our common stream,

the one who turned too often in the net
and strangled on its joy;
yet still the one who whispers to me
of our human pain
when the salmon burst like flashbulbs
every spring along the coast
in a brilliant consecration
of the undeveloped souls who journey here

TIM BOWLING

Venus Time

> *"The period of rotation, 224 Earth days, is the slowest of all the planets and is longer than the period of the planet's revolution, so that Venus' day is about ten per cent longer than its year."*
>
> — a science textbook

In your absence, everything is motionless
and it is my pain, not the sun or the earth
or the nine satellites of Saturn,
that is the centre of the universe.
Even astronomers of the sixteenth century,
Copernican irreverents holding quadrants
to their widening gaze, predicted
that your star would burst
and leave my planet cold: later,
Kepler with his eyes still sore
from telescopic staring at the sun
wrote in fiery red letters
through his gauze of tears
of a cataclysm due to fall,
and Galileo, dropping lead and feathers
from Pisa's Leaning Tower, knew
that all the heavens changed
only when one chose to see them change

I haven't made that choice

Ptolemaic to the bone, I still insist
your orbit is around me, in a space
so infinite and beautiful it contains
all knowledge and all truth;
I have burned every other life
for treason at the stake,
I have ground the strongest lenses
into dust for the solar winds
to scatter as they will;
my firmament, my faith, is fixed

Yet here, now, among the few objects
you left behind, the records and the books,
a lipstick burning on the bathroom vanity
red as Mars, all the nebulae of dissolution,
I know what it means to live on Venus time,
growing ancient by the hour, weak and frail,
pointing obsolete instruments at a just-discovered world

The Lesson

Anthony is standing outside his bedroom, calling
for help. For the past few minutes he has tried
to turn his t-shirt around after the initial mistake

of putting it on with the decal backwards,
and all he has been able to do is straightjacket
his left arm helplessly between his shoulderblades,

while his right hand hangs from the collar, twitching
like a broken wing. He is breathing hard, a sweaty sheen
to his cheeks, but he tries again, twisting and writhing

like a magician struggling to get unstrapped from
a mismanaged trick, eyes closed like a saint overwhelmed
by a rapture that grips him by the body and won't let go.

William Fledderus

The Journey of the Unutukait

for Pam and Steve Martin

"A cold coming we had of it,
the ice was rough and cruel.
We decided to skip Pangnirtung and
take an inland route,
but country food was scarce
and we went hungry a few days.
It was December, and the sun only showed his face
three or four hours a day.
Nights with these two old walruses
made me long for Geela's body
and the old bed we shared back home.
My oldest kid has that bed now —
last time I saw it was when his wife Elisipee
gave birth to my nephew Joey.

"In Iqualuit we stocked up
and I saw my cousin Malektoo
who drives a sewage truck.
We were glad to see each other.
Everybody calls me Mike, Paulasi,
except for you, he said.
I told him I had heard Tommy was in trouble.
(Tommy is my younger brother).
He pointed down towards the flow edge:
Tommy's shacked up with a
hooker named Lily. Be careful —
he even threatened to shoot
the priest a few weeks ago.
Tommy's place was an un-
insulated shack.
A pregnant white answered the door
and said he was out hunting caribou
three days northeast. Did she need anything,
I asked. (No heat was coming out the door).

The baby is due next week, she told me,
her expression struggling
between fierceness and tenderness.

"We didn't have to go far out of our way
to catch up with Tommy.
He didn't say he was glad to see us.
He hadn't got any caribou because
he'd chased a good-sized polar bear
for a day and a half, he said.
With what, I asked.
He pointed to his rifle.
I told him he was a fool
and that he'd better get home before
Lily brought his child into the world alone.
I'm afraid of that child, he said.
He'll be a good-for-nothing half-breed.
I told Malaiyah and Gita to go home,
because I was going back
to stay with Tommy and Lily for a few days.
They said they would like to come too,
if that was okay — lots of food in the sled.

"We saw the smoke before we actually got there.
The place was in flames, burning like a beacon.
Half the town was there, milling about.
Nobody was trying to put the fire out.
They were just staring. The way it blazed
it looked like it would never be consumed.

"All this was long ago. I'm setting it down on paper
because that shack is haunting my dreams,
burning, never going out. When I wake up
I sometimes catch a whiff of
the sweet fragrance of sacrifice in my nostrils."

Elyse Yates St. George

Ungava Bay, 1991

three women went a hunting and now are dead
marrow bone and flesh a stone
that sprouts

ice filigree
intricate as lichen
white on white pervasive

as the storm they tried to walk away from
their snowmobile stalled
past point of no return

walked the night half-carrying a boy
the searchers later found alive — that small hunter
who'd tagged along eager

with his first gun a rifle he cannot hold now
with stumps of fingers frost bit off — after
the women left him sealed in snow

wrapped in caribou hide
a shroud around him not knowing
any of the possible truths

Ann Goldring

The Pigeon, Icarus

Each night at six the man opens
the small doors of cages for pigeons
to flutter out into sun-painted skies. One
by one they reel off their perch, strike their wings
into beating, collect in clouds sweeping together
sculpting skyways
banked for rising and falling, slicing light
white to silver
grey to silver

Each night I pedal my bike, watch
the birds not the road. I want to be one of them
rustling up eddies to cross and
crisscross, until the sky is tangled in currents
so next when we plunge through we stop sailing
together but, like coins skytossed in reckless abandon
we jangle and muddle our pretty precision. I wonder

why night after night they forfeit their freedom
return to their cages, settle softly in darkness
muffle longing in attics for what they gave up.

Would I?

Or you, if given the chance (if the wax didn't melt)

work waived, obligations cancelled — we've quite done
enough — would we return to our cages each night
coo each other to sleep dreaming

of flight?

John B. Lee

The Whistler Swans in My Father's Fields

This spring
they'd landed there in the thousands
like the snow that lay
where it falls
or melts a little
against the black
and darkens the soil, seeping
like water in cloth:
black till
white swans
calling themselves down
like the far cry of children
playing behind buildings
in the closed echo
of some inner square.

And they stay a week
and then a second
the way grandmothers keep lonely vigil
in daughters' kitchens
the tea kettle whistling
two half steps from the table
the rain
catching against the window
like a soft-clawed cat
climbing glass
saying "how is it I can't reach the world
I'm looking at?
Why is it I can't touch
into and through this invisible stillness
to the action beyond."

And then Jan and I
are driving
west of Aylmer
where the hawks outdistance
our own expectations of flight
by gliding
like the feathered silence
that comes on the verge of sleep . . .
that same kind of slow passage
the trees manage at dusk
or the slip of tide
shushing down pebbles and shells
until they're still
and settled the way gravity
wishes they were
and she says then
"in the woods
you can smell the deer"
and she means
more than must and scat
more like the oak in wine
seasoned by wood.
And I say, "Yes"
I can smell them
beyond the radio light
and ashy scent
in the cramped chrysalis of the cars.
It's something like
having an ear on your chin
and owling for the movement of mice.
Something like stroking the moon
with your back
and seeing your shadow shape
shutter the entire thirty miles
across a quiet lake.

Lear at Stratford

"So we'll live,
and pray, and sing, and tell old tales,
and laugh at gilded butterflies . . ."

— Shakespeare,
King Lear

Lear at Stratford
meant a long drive
up a November highway
leafy with rain,
and only my younger brother
came with me in the car.

If anything, a stormy night was right — for Lear.
We chatted on about the play:
the moors, the madness, things that people say
. . . or don't inside a family.

We seemed easy together, there alone
as the road wore on, turning back our minds
to times when we were both at home;
his small adventures as a boy.

I hadn't known, 'till then,
how much our hurt and loss
had made a silence of those years
before our father died — the kitchen table times —
a silence of my brother's childhood.
How eager he had been to hear
the stories I had shut away like a keepsake box.

Beside me, in the dark, he had
a man's voice that I had heard before:
soft cadences and laughter.
I knew the play, and knew Cordelia now,
her love more ponderous than her tongue.

Patricia Young

The Origins of the Kiss

I wish to speak of origins:
the snail's caress, its antennae and the roots
growing deep in the earth. I wish
to speak of the duck's bill, guillemots nibbling
each others' feet, the pose of any feathered thing.
I have traced the kiss
to Semitic antiquity, beyond Africa
and her asexual wild grasses! Homer scarcely knew it,
the Greek poets seldom mentioned the kiss
though it took the rest of Europe
by surprise. In Lapland
the kiss was considered the centre
of gravity, to be planted
just below the navel
where, they said, a pool
of sex-water lies. In Celtic tongues
there was no word for kiss and so I sat alone
in a farmhouse trying to invent
a name. The Welsh kissed
only on special occasions, at a game called
carousal. Whenever there is rope-playing there is also
moonlight and then one came to me,
shaped like a beet or pear.
Through eastern Asia
the kiss was unknown, in Japanese literature
pleasure was intense. The kiss has always been alive
in the dreams of schizophrenics, reveries
of satyrs — a theta wave
in the alchemist's brain. During lovemaking
the Tamils licked each other's eyelids.
I wish to speak of such tenderness, the wisdom
derived by voluptuous acts. In the light
of Palestine the kiss grew
in the incandescent
spaces between olive trees.

Among early Christians: of sacramental significance —
kiss the relic of a saint, foot of the pope.
In Rome the kiss was a sign of reverence
and so the erotic possibilities
did not become flesh.
Was it
the terrible kiss of God
that caused the virgins of central Russia to lose
consciousness and turn
into dock leaves? In Borneo, nose-pressing
was the kiss of welcome and
of mourning. Arabian deities
were easily uncaged
when about to
receive them. Powerful
the impulse and yet the Chinese thought it
cannibalistic. Among the hill tribes
of India: olfactory, nose to cheek,
smell me, they said.
Mothers of the Niger coast rubbed their babies
with their lips, lovers did not.
And the great,
unlit kiss that feeds on mud at the bottom
of the lake — that ancient and primitive
longing! I wish to speak
of the mammal's bite and the hunger
inside me. For every human infant.
Watch them claim their world,
their small fists
bringing each detail
up to
their mouths.

Letter in Flight

Piano tuner missing over Pacific hanging from 32
helium balloons
— Japanese transport ministry spokesman

If I have ceased to trust words, who can blame me?
So long I've been riding this wooden crate —
poorly equipped and tossed in the air like a buoyant cup.

The night before my journey our telephone
rang blue as your favorite
shirt. I stopped
my ears, disdained all warnings.
I would not listen to coast guards or government
officials, their feet buried deep
in the Kanto plain.

You were not watching when I lifted off
I was a tangle of strings. I shouted to the crowd,
how pleased I was with my bird's eye view.
And higher — the islands arcing
northward, the Roof of Hokkaido.

From you I took little.
Only the rice cakes you packed in an old biscuit tin,
the wool blanket your brother gave as a wedding gift.

The balloons above me are rotund angels.
Each one six metres wide. You would think such lightness
could carry me across a thousand
copper seas and yet
I have not reached California.

The first days I waved my arms at sandhill
cranes, small aircraft; anything that flew
became my friend but now the sky
is too vast and I am lonely for the beginning
and end of a day. For our daughter,
the way she would hold
for a moment my face in her hands.
And you, sometimes sweeping the porch
when I returned in the evening with my bag
of small hammers, my tuning forks.

Keiko, I forgive you everything.
For loving me too much and then not enough.

On postcards I scribble short
prayers before tossing them into the waves.

The wind pushes me like a hammock.

The world is a dark hood and I pull it

over my eyes.

Yoshikazu.

PATRICIA YOUNG

Pinantan Lake: The Summer the Marriage Comes Apart

Hot sheets in the wind, your hands
moving down my body. Have they always moved
this way, as though they understand
something has died?

Beside the bed, two mangoes
and a jug of ice water. After we roll apart
I lie beside you thinking: so
that's what it's like to make love
to a man whose soul
is not in it.

The lake is loon-filled, fluted with cries.
Beyond the blue spruce someone is shouting
over and over: *love, you say love, well sweetheart I ain't seen*
any of that around here
for thirty years.

A white saucer-moon breaks into the mess of reeds.
I stand on the balcony, the mosquitoes
avoiding my blood as though *I*
have the plague.

He's drunk, come back inside, you say, and begin
to dream: we are dancing, in step
at last, and then I am
dancing with a man who
looks like you, only younger, he is wearing
a yellow shirt, a Latin band is playing
tango after tango, almost midnight,
the crowd wild as Mardi Gras.

And what do I dream? That you are kissing
Ineke, my mother's neighbour, her husband, the landscape
gardener, is sitting on a couch gripping the hoe
across his knees, I keep trying
to tear you from the Dutch woman, *good god, look*
at his face, I say, pulling you toward the front
door, *let's get our shoes*, but they are
cut-throat trout swimming just below
the surface. *Soulless*, you say,
reaching into the murk.
Soulless, I say, scooping out mine.

SUSAN MCMASTER

The Gardener's Dream

I lay you on the bed
of grass
cut carefully with my sod knife
around your shape
with each of your
small cries
reach under, cut free
one sliver of turf
with its skein of root,
one blade of grass,
cut and lift, place
it a small green flame
on your uncovered skin,
for each of your
sighs
lift, and plant
one more blade,
one more green light
till round your form
the grass flames green,
the earth below
freed blade by blade
of its cover, loosens,
grows rich, grows warm,
a bed hollowed deep
from your hollow cries

The last blade I place
with its crumble of soil
its gleaming leaf
on your still perfect forehead
then lift myself, lay
my gardener's tired body
on the mound of your greenly
flaming skin

press you
blanket you
between earth and sod

garden you in

For Tomatoes

One hot tomato
with its prickly top,
its round and sexy middle,
its unexpected, thorny center:
This tomato seeing me would see itself,
like one from another planet
would recognize a life.
It knows my kind,
slices of our future, present, past,
mixing you and me with many others
and by the body remembering
the vulnerable seed,
the hard green adolescence
and the raw red language of the adult.

Looking at the tomato
I too see endless, red slices,
then one in particular
cut by my mother at the beach —
warm, sandy, immeasurably good.
Afterward the rides at Crystal Beach Park,
one called The Whirling Devil,
a giant, rotating barrel painted deep red.
And me as it began its slow turn,
mixing in my mind the machine
with the beach tomato,
spinning faster and faster
the centrifugal force pushing,
the blood red floor falling away,
my brain hot juice.
So still the motion I was
the red walls themselves,
only a slight dizziness away
from absolute pleasure.

We took the wrong subway, stepped
out into a vacant air
a woman told us was Harlem.
It was quiet there.
As we walked through the streets
and Needle Park, I couldn't understand
the word ghetto
and what it didn't mean that morning.
The emptied streets, the park
and the trees where a man
walked his dogs in the last days
of summer, the two men
on the stairs as we passed,
who hardly glanced
at our edgy flight.

Caught in a storm
that night in the Village,
we sat in a restaurant,
talked ourselves tired
and it wasn't just lightning
turning the night sky to fire
that cracked open our lives.
It was the layers of dust
that wouldn't wash from my skin.
Godard's *Breathless*
in the stale, dank theatre.
Starry Night's thick pigments
behind heavy glass, each
brushstroke an etching
of open desire. The few birds
in Needle Park chattering
in the green heat. The rain falling
like it could scrub the streets clean.

Neile Graham

Tomb of the Eagles

for Ronald and Morgan Simison

I'm left-handed like her — the child
who made this shard, who shaping a pot
marked its rim with the knife of her thumbnail,

the etch etch etch of her hand on red clay
then the vessel shattered with her grandparents'
clean bones and with her own. Her knife fits

in my fingers perfect like bones.
She carried it close. I can feel her hands fitting
where my fingers do, rubbing the notched edge.

Morgan Simison's palms slide over a skull
browned with 5,000 years of burial, workworn hands
trace the shape of the strap on the top

of her head, my mothers' mother, misshapen
by the weight of fuel, food, child.
A life of hard work for a simple meal.

But among the bones no sign of murder —
survival enough violence for them all.
The blunt affection of her hands on the skull.

She loves what she knows of these long-dead folk,
the shape of the lands her husband and children till.
The tomb her husband uncovered built of generations

of hands that knew these cliffs, this soil.
The stories we can't guess, why the bones
of sea-eagles mix with their dead.

I want to shape the child's name, whatever words
she had for bowl and knife and the ragged sea
below the cliffs of her tribe's tomb,

the seal swimming along among the rocks,
whatever words she would use for the way my thumb
fits into the prints of her own.

Susan Goyette

Confessions

1

The student body snaked its way
to a folded ping-pong table.
A priest sat behind it
listening to confessions
in a gym that stank of sweat and sneakers
and sin.
I could hear kids whispering,
  say you pushed your sister —
  forgot to say your prayers.

I'd prayed every night all week,
please God of everlasting love
and lambs,
please give me something to confess
and a barbie camper.

2

I confess mother,
the night I told you I was sleeping at Mary's
I was star-splayed
under a summer night sky
with the sweetest cloud covering me.

Nestled on rusty pine needles
and gnarled old roots,
I made snow-angels in July,
suction cupped myself like a star fish
to him.

I also confess,
my plant you watered
wasn't a tomato.
You wondered why it kept shrinking
and why I kept coming
home later and later.

That summer I was guiltier
than grass stains.

3

Alone in his apartment
I searched through my ex-lover's poems,
wanting to read the ones with my name
and breasts again.
I wasn't surprised to see
he had whited out my name
but hadn't touched my body.

Some nights I wake and find
a pillow between my legs
and I leave it there,
still hearing his voice
hard as verbs.
I'm warm with want,
dreaming of being his sentence.

4

There are days
when the rain's drilling
drives holes in my body,
deeper than my bones.
And I write,
umbrella umbrella UMBRELLA.
Getting colder and wetter
each line.

5

I always lost count
doing penance.
Always did one more
for the road.

Karen Massey

Bus Shelter, 2 a.m.

She walks out of the rain, slow-singing some blue country
song, its down-home twang sounding not half bad. She tucks
into the shelter where I'm standing alone, her clothes
stained with weather. She turns to face me with dark eyes,
cigarette-smoke scented breath, and I see it clearly:
blue-green bruise, like the shadow of a hand-slap across her
face, its four fingers fanning outward across one cheek.
Just like that she says, "I know what you're thinking, but it
ain't right." I'm looking down at the platform, scuffing my
shoe against the metal floor, casual. "My angel flew too
close — brushed a wing against my face," she says slowly,
distinctly. "Even my angel ain't perfect," she tells me,
"Must've got confused." Then she starts back humming that
tune, and I think I recognize it, blending in so nice with
the sad slap of rain on the street.

Gary Hyland

Recitin From a Feelin: Robert Johnson

1

Stepdaddy Dusty Willis:
Couldn't get that boy one day behind no mule,
nothin for him but cheap music and cheatin school.

R. L. Windum:
I jus trifled for a time, you understan,
but Robert he studied them blues,
tanned his fingers learnin
Charlie Patton, Whiskey Red, Son House.
Studied Ike Zinnerman
who usedta sit on tombstones
just to get the feel.

Johnny Shines:
I'd work on Robert's moves but it was like a snake
tryin to ride a bicycle. He did these diminished
sixths and sevenths, these miracle runs, even was
plannin to mix in piano, bass and drums. Who knows
what music that boy mighta made he'da lived to thirty.
I swear he have three brains, four hands
and more licks than a stump fulla puppies.

This one time some one o' the reglars in Detroit asks
Robert play that crusher he played a few nights back
and Robert says, "It's gone. I was jus' recitin from a feelin."

2

Corrie Craft:
I'da gone with him myself, my sister hadn't,
so dapper an' so sad. He come honest to the blues —
his share of leavin an' bein left,
wife, baby dead, his natural father
stayin disappeared all his life. Most to killed his heart
that an' leavin Callie and the kids.

Honey Boy Edwards:
Weren't too many Delta women never heard of R.J.
What he's do soons we'd hit Tchula, Walls, Beulah,
Midnight, Lamont, some such place, Robert'd scout him
the homeliest witch in town, spread some honey on her.
Have himself a sugar nest anytime he want.

3

Corrie Craft:
Shot dead from a Midnight woman
he done two-timed once too much.

Rev. Tooley Rivers:
Counterfeit, all them other deaths,
cause I seen him go two years later
in Kansas City at the Blue Match Club.

He was playin the same corruption
when he was snatched right off his stool
by the flamin hand of Satan himself.

Stackhouse Houston:
The way I gathered it is that Saturday night
in Greenwood Robert has too many eyes all over
the houseman's wife and there was talk she and him
was patchin' down all week. And so during a break
some fellas offer Robert a half-pint with a broken seal
and he puts away most if it before he goes back on.

First he's too pained to sing but the crowd wants more
so he tries and plays sick awhile and then collapses.
Houseman dosed that drink with strychnine, you see,
and it took him to pneumonia and that's what took him off.

Honey Boy Edwards:
Jimson weed in that jug
and they slung him to town
and I don't know why
they kept him in a shack
without no doctor
and he was snappin and growlin
three entire days
before it ended.

His Half-Sister:
My mama who was Robert's mama
never told me my little brother was dead
County buried him in a two dollar box.
His Daddy's name on the death certificate
markin him a bastard, my little brother.

Mama say that day the sky was unnatural
still. Like them roadhouse crowds
when almost in blood
he finished singing.

The Clowns Are Dying All Over the World their Faces

the clowns are dying all over the world their faces
ajar luminous as dials under their wigs charred cogs
winch down never again will this story be told as if
it were the first one wingspan of eyebrows to rout
the sky an uncivil joy of clowns leaked somewhere
between synapse a seizure of small wheels in the end
gaunt men spit in palms sweep from the ring a little
muddle of sawdust & zinc a smile split to fruit the
windfall of glance gone bad on the branch who cares
not i said the dead clown shucking skin whatever falls
out of my head falls into my pocket and reaches into
antique cage of rib to wind the clockwork bird that
squalls him carnal again blowing worlds like balloons
ardent and green

Plover Crying

Dark night —
plover crying
for its nest.

— Basho,
On Love and Barley

The lost nest
floats by me
on its way.

The Limpopo, the Mississippi, the Danube
or, following the Nile
to the salty mouth
of the Mediterranean,
it holds in its twigged lap
my other child.

Where sturdy waters, oxbows, or tributaries
can map but circumstantial paths,
the nest knows the best way
to carry its small self,
a round obelisk navigating
through depths
it's not concerned with.

And I can only wonder
who would make this sea-bound cradle
with me in mind? Who was the mother,
gone from her laying?
That wise bird,
who traded the river
for the full dry air,

trusting lost things
will have a continence
all their own.

The Visitor

The gallery is warm. No breath of wind.
Three perfumed ladies
leave their scent behind and move on.

On the soft brown carpet
the visitor stands alone
to one side:
a woman of uncertain age
holding a child.

Her gentle hands
are carelessly supportive;
seemingly, her thoughts are
elsewhere.

The paintings on the walls
the shapes of the sculptures
do not
command her attention.

what she sees
is snow:

> newly drifted snow
> first snow
> spreading snow
> drifting snow
> beating snow
> salty snow
> watery snow
> soft snow
> drinkable snow
> building snow

In her language there are
twenty-three
different words for snow.

She has travelled a long way
to this
temperature-and-humidity-controlled
art
gallery.

> *Glorious it is to see*
> *The caribou flocking down from the forests*
> *And beginning*
> *Their wandering . . .*

The gallery is warm.
No breath of wind.
Three perfumed ladies
leave their scent behind
and move on.

On the soft brown carpet
the visitor stands alone
to one side:

> *Inuit sculpture: Mother and Child*
> *by Kakasilala of Cape Dorset N.W.T.*
> *(please do not touch)*

Note: "Glorious it is to see . . ." is by Netsik of the Canadian Inuit, one of the Inuit poems recorded and translated by visiting anthropologists at the beginning of this century.

David Manicom

Radiation

(a Betty Goodwin triptych, for D.B.)

1
(The Swimmers)

As if in love you might "burrow into the gesture"
Their drowning bodies in this revealed transparency
Are not themselves entirely opaque, the torsos starred
Like old lenses and marred within by odd incisions, dust.
The instrument is absent: lust, or the painter's brush
And nervous grip. See thus only what is left behind,
Cancerous, the disease nothing of itself, a blind stir,
Its former presence afterward inferred, a door
No one has seen opened by no one passing through
Into the avenue of doors, a swift inanimacy.

You wrote to me capering a thinking cap of flesh,
"Our best skinhead poet," a lovely, bragging terror.
I felt the first rift in the fields of gravity.
My mother has her hands in water, apron tied.
Her husband pulls the laces of his workboots tight.
Our crazy neighbour cycles madly after trains.
My lover sighs beneath the heavens in the shower.
Your craftsman double-stitches canvas for an arctic night.
Goodwin dims the studio to ease her unbelief,
The swimmers strain to hover in their painted light.

2
(Seated Figure With Red Angle)

"They are seeking a place to breathe, trying to move out."
In my bereft returning unto you the bodies float
Like notes of piano music in a basement flat,
God's transparencies, a colour wash, the density
Of flesh that is deepest at the skin. Concavity stilled.

The windowsills well daylight on your upper walls
So far as I can see, my phone call never getting through,
Your hand floating into the view toward the endless ring,
Lesion of your piano playing silenced, raw umber
Part of ivory. I check and re-check the number.

My pure intentions as an underwater line
Between two continents, but it is signs and passages
To *the outside* — not a salvaged intimacy —
You need from me now. My voice, a wire in the canvas,
The swimmers in their final genius contemplate
As just another self-assuring artifact. Yellow
Of cadmium on my palette still, dialling hopelessly,
Sparely tinging white and gathering about the throat
A thickening frottage of cadmium red.
You resume your music. There are no lines in it, or out.

3

(Figure With Chair)

The will, you said, turns "Not in the leaving of traces,
But in using what is left to continue," the will
You said, as an eraser like a season
Worked inside the vigour of your figure, into black clouds
And tailings, brute diagonal strokes as if
Some fundamental chair, the very seat of airs
Tipped slowly, a declension of the word *fear*.
There is thickening at the nape, a collar of war.
Inside, the scraping leaves but shallows of your plans,
And is that another, smaller head, cringing near the heart?

And so the forward pressure, like a purchased debt,
That sense of slippage, of the angles drawn
for the new arrangement of the coat, the toys,
The pillow and the key. Do your hips press forward,
A shoulder turning in the gladed light, eyes lifting
But never quite to bear? The sound of a knife
Scraping dry toast. You? You could rise at night
And find a stranger standing in the shadowed hall,
Not like a dream but as if there are no dreams.

Denise Cammiade

Chimeral Dark

We had been camping down the coast;
sprawled beside a fire with some friends
we talked of Santa Cruz and Port San Luis
joked about our eeyore of a van.
Our voices, like firelight exploded up
then dropped back cool into dark.
High and fluting then
we heard the sound of bats;
siren music.
Their velvet bodies shuttled, veered from a line of trees to the sea
looped the sky.

We went for one last swim
sleekly phosphorescent we
went a long way out that night, so warm.

Stroking back to land through foil-bright water
our limbs shimmered, silver
they emerged, descended in glistening arcs.
Perfect, that night, that sea.
And we
perfectly tired, reached shore.
Diamonds fell from our skin.

Tonight, I set the thermostat,
let our hunting tom outside to prowl
(a gulp of winter hurries through the door)
lights out, you help me tug my slip above my shoulders.
It crackles with static
explodes
— a small fission of sparkles.

In this dark season we jump back, take pleasure in this hint
this brief surprise.

Denise Cammiade

Instrumental Sestina

Sometimes I think of your hands
picture them close to wood
the curve of your fingers holding the capable
tools: your fragile chisels, those Japanese saws you bought in your travels
the way you stroked woodgrain, the wordless knowing
then skimmed off layers, stripped rosewood of all but its naked music

You eased together lutes, violins, guitars; anything that made music
sculpted soundboards fine as snowflakes. There was deftness in those hands
certainty like trees themselves their knowing
dark earth, white seasons. You were at home with wood
let it carry you, like sap that travels
turpentine-pungent, clean to the capable

sky. Your amber mind capable
of anything. Well, anything, it seemed, except the music
of everyday life. Always those restless travels
at a moment's notice. The way you caught my hands
said your were leaving. No date, no address. Words like wood
the sawed-off scraps, kicked pointedly between us. Knowing

together, jolting apart. Weeks, months; me never knowing
where you'd be tomorrow. Wishing I were capable
of the placidness of wood
content to wait in corners for the music
of footsteps. I hadn't the sweet-scented patience, feared rough justice, hands
of landlords. Couldn't lie smoothly, dream of the ends of fingers or travels

Too many hours. Left. And still my mind travels
backward to greet you. Amnesiac memory, as if never knowing
cobwebs or gaps. I touch other hands
their disparate fingers. Wonder if they are capable
of reading the intricate music
brailled in the cells of any held thing? My body turned to wood

far from your grasp. The days, a black wood
peopled by strangers. I travel
them mutely, mind wanders off, goes to find music.
Lately, it happens so often I've stopped even knowing
the roads I've walked past. If time is capable
of healing, why is the only tune I remember the song of your hands?

Since hollow things float symphonies of music
I should be capable of any theme; rinded like wood
by the spell of travelling hands.

Wayne Gabriel

Home : a Glose

> *If you're stronghearted ripple your way*
> *up and down over low green-patched hills.*
> *You can look from twenty feet and be unobserved*
> *except for the fire of your eyes.*
>
> — Milton Acorn
> "Dig up my heart"

I can take you there,
we could walk the storm
tossed beach at daybreak,
watch the ocean's fingers
carve their slow pass
between the rocks all day
then turn our tracks, head where
the trail cuts the edge and we must lean out
to follow our sun-stretched shadows on the bay
and if you're stronghearted ripple your way.

We won't go back the way
we came, we'll take the long path,
that winds between
cropped and twisted spruce
where they hug the ledge like gnarled old men
leaning on window sills;
where birds rest against the chill
snuggled down for fragile warmth,
kept safe as the wind shrills
up and down over low green-patched hills

and if you like the wind's
wild song and dance, then come
with me to the cliff face
where we can see the beach
stretch out forty? fifty feet?
before it's curved.
We can climb down, build a fire in the sand
and I know where we could lie in love
alone and undisturbed
where you can look from twenty feet and be unobserved.

I would tell you
these secrets I hold
and every reason I possess
for taking you here
where only dying waves and wind
can hear my nurtured cries
and I would tell you
how it doesn't matter
no, nothing matters here, even lies,
nothing, except for the fire of your eyes.

7:16

I have never written of your death.
Never written of that swaying train
where every man in narrow aisle after aisle rubbed against me
while I swore and bullied past,
swung my heavy backpack, glared at the
corridors of leering faces, but could only think of you.

For a moment, all of Portugal became you.
Every swarthy face took on your mask of death,
so transparent I could almost see your skull amongst the
tangled map of oxygen and I.V. tubes. The train
slowed and whistled shrilly as Lisbon swept past
and everywhere I looked, my eyes deceived me.

My friend, your face startled me.
Alone in Portugal that dusky night, I knew you
had gone. Your ghost flew past.
In every building, foreign face, I felt the dizzying of death.
The station clock said 7:16 when I arrived, the train
on time, even here, the slowest country in the

world. A world that spun an extra revolution on the
day you travelled halfway round to visit me,
a death in Canada at Portuguese twilight, and then your image in that train.
The sight of you, so frail, made me weep with losing you.
It was difficult enough, leaving months before your death,
your stubborn insistence that the past

wasn't a place for me to live. You never held me to our past:
early attempts at love, those fragile roots that grew like weeds, the
bewildering of life. No thoughts of death
back then. No thoughts until you challenged me
to travel as we'd planned, to carry on without you.
For that I let you die while I was far away, a foreign train,

weeks of mourning on a lonely shore, trying to train
myself to realize you were gone. After the first week, events of the past
Sunday already surreal, I phoned your parents and we spoke of you
in the past tense. That was the hardest thing I think. The
wind burning my face, summer headlong toward me
and nothing to hold onto but your death.

Your death will always be that dirty train, the
grime of Lisbon station, clock at sixteen minutes past, and me
at last a foreigner to you, startling and clear and full of death.